CLIMATE CHANGE:
Can Humanity Adapt?

Andrea C. Nakaya

San Diego, CA

For more information, contact:
ReferencePoint Press, Inc.
PO Box 27779
San Diego, CA 92198
www.ReferencePointPress.com

LIBRARY OF CONGRESS CATALOGING-IN-PUBLICATION DATA

Names: Nakaya, Andrea C., 1976- author.
Title: Climate change : can humanity adapt? / by Andrea C. Nakaya.
Description: San Diego, CA : ReferencePoint Press, 2025. | Includes bibliographical references and index.
Identifiers: LCCN 2024051659 (print) | LCCN 2024051660 (ebook) | ISBN 9781678210700 (library binding) | ISBN 9781678210717 (ebook)
Subjects: LCSH: Climate change adaptation. | Global environmental change. | Environmental policy.
Classification: LCC GF71 .N353 2025 (print) | LCC GF71 (ebook) | DDC 304.2/8--dc23/eng/20250109
LC record available at https://lccn.loc.gov/2024051659
LC ebook record available at https://lccn.loc.gov/2024051660

CONTENTS

Adapting to Climate Change: A Critical Challenge

Extreme heat is one of the most dangerous consequences of climate change. According to the World Health Organization, it kills close to five hundred thousand people worldwide every year, and that number is growing. Las Vegas is just one city where the threat of extreme heat is becoming more severe. In 2024, *New York Times* writers Ronda Kaysen and Aatish Bhatia researched heat there, analyzing weather data and interviewing residents and scientists. They found that average summer temperatures have increased steadily over the years and have become dangerous. Kaysen and Bhatia report that in July 2024, Las Vegas saw temperatures reach 120°F (49°C), which was the hottest ever recorded there. In addition, they state that during June and July, nighttime temperatures rarely dropped lower than 79°F (26°C). When temperatures stay high at night, the heat is even more dangerous because people's bodies have no time to recover from it. The human body does not handle extreme heat well, and when it gets hot enough for long enough, people start to die.

Seventy-four-year-old retired blackjack dealer Anita Swogger was among the victims of the 2024 heat in Las Vegas. She lived in East Las Vegas, where summer temperatures are generally above 100°F (38°C). After her air-conditioning broke in June, her son Tristan found her dead on her bathroom floor. Experts guess that because the bathroom had poor ventilation, it was probably much hotter than elsewhere in her home. Swogger had been waiting for a new air-conditioning unit to be installed in just a few days. "It was horrible, just horrible timing,"[1] says Tristan. Las Vegas is one example of how a changing climate is becoming a serious threat to people's health and well-being. As the climate continues to change and people face a growing number of threats, more are wondering whether humanity will be able to successfully adapt.

Climate Change Is Happening Now

The climate is changing everywhere, and it poses a serious threat to humanity. The world is experiencing higher temperatures, rising sea levels, droughts, degraded water quality, new disease threats, increased extreme weather events, and many other issues that impact life on land and in the oceans. These transformations have been documented by scientists around the world, with many expressing alarm at the rapid pace of change.

The National Aeronautics and Space Administration (NASA) explains that climate change poses a new and significant challenge for humankind. Earth's climate has changed before, but the last major climate upheaval was thousands of years ago, which means humanity has become deeply dependent on current environmental conditions. "Earth's climate has been relatively stable for the past 10,000 years, and this stability has allowed for the development of our modern civilization and agriculture," explains NASA. "Our modern life is tailored to that stable climate." Now that stability is disappearing, and the potential consequences are significant for all of humanity. As NASA warns, "Climate change . . . has been at least partly responsible for the rise and fall of civilizations."[2]

"Climate change . . . has been at least partly responsible for the rise and fall of civilizations."[2]

—National Aeronautics and Space Administration

Adaptation Is Essential

To survive in this changing climate, humanity will need to adapt. Adaptation is the process of taking action to prepare for and adjust

People use umbrellas to block the sun during a July 2024 heat wave in Las Vegas, Nevada. Average summer temperatures in Las Vegas have increased, and dangerous heat has become more common there.

to the impacts of climate change. The goal of adaptation is to help individuals and communities become less vulnerable to the changes they are currently facing and those they will face in the future. It includes a range of different actions and policies, from individual behavior to large government projects. The United Nations Framework Convention on Climate Change (UNFCCC) explains:

> Adaptation actions can take on many forms, depending on the unique context of a community, business, organization, country or region. There is no "one-size-fits-all-solution"—adaptation can range from building flood defences, setting up early warning systems for cyclones, switching to drought-resistant crops, to redesigning communication systems, business operations and government policies.[3]

Just as climate change is already happening, so is adaptation. Humanity is currently taking many actions to adapt to problems that are already unfolding. For example, some communities have built seawalls to protect themselves from rising water levels, and others have created new building designs that will help people stay cooler during heat waves. Other adaptation efforts are focused on future challenges, like managing water in areas that are likely to experience drought. Around the world, people have seen both successes and challenges when it comes to these efforts. Many innovative solutions have been found to some of the problems caused by climate change, but it is generally agreed that more must be done.

> **"Adaptation actions can take on many forms, depending on the unique context of a community, business, organization, country or region. There is no 'one-size-fits-all-solution.'"[3]**
>
> —United Nations Framework Convention on Climate Change

Adaptation is widely recognized as essential for humanity's survival. NASA explains that even if worldwide efforts to reduce emissions to slow climate change are successful, it will still be necessary to adapt to changing conditions. "Even if we stopped emitting all greenhouse gases today, global warming and climate change will continue to affect future generations," it says. "In this way, humanity is 'committed' to some level of climate change."[4] This means that, like it or not, humanity must commit to some level of adaptation.

Why Does Humanity Need to Adapt?

Tens of thousands of Americans relocate every year. They are driven by many reasons, such as for a new job or to be closer to friends or family. For a growing number, however, climate change is a major motivation to move. For instance, worsening wildfires due to the changing climate are what drove Roy Parvin and his wife, Janet Vail, to relocate 2,600 miles (4,184 km), from Cloverdale, California, to Asheville, North Carolina. After experiencing numerous wildfires, they left in 2020 after one came within a quarter mile of their house. "We left . . . after getting tired of being evacuated in the middle of the night by a policeman saying, 'Pack your cars, take your dogs, don't pick up anything, just go,'"[5] says Parvin.

Like Parvin and Vail, more and more people are realizing that their communities are irrevocably changing because of climate change. In the United States, a 2023 survey by the Pew Research Center found that 41 percent of people believe that over the next thirty years climate change will make their community a worse place to live. Rather than continuing to suffer from the negative effects and increasing threats, they are attempting to make a change—to adapt.

The Climate Is Changing

Twenty years ago, there was widespread debate over climate change. Some people insisted it was happening, but others contended that the evidence was inconclusive. Today, however, climate change—which is primarily caused by human-generated greenhouse gas emissions—is widely accepted as a fact. The United Nations Development Programme (UNDP) explains that Earth is 1.9°F (1.1°C) warmer now that it was in the 1800s, prior to the Industrial Revolution. This might not sound like a lot, but that small temperature increase is having dramatic impacts on the world. The UNDP explains, "This warming is causing widespread and rapid changes in our planet's atmosphere, ocean and ecosystems."[6] It warns that within this century, the world is on track for an increase of 4.5°F to 5.2°F (2.5°C to 2.9°C) above preindustrial levels. Most scientists believe that a temperature increase of this size will have massive impacts on the climate, altering life as we know it in fundamental ways.

> **"Warming is causing widespread and rapid changes in our planet's atmosphere, ocean and ecosystems."[6]**
>
> —United Nations Development Programme

Weather and temperature patterns are changing and becoming more unpredictable, and both heat waves and droughts are more common. Extreme weather events like storms are also becoming more likely, and they cause more damage when they occur. In addition, as global temperatures rise, glaciers and sea ice are melting, and sea levels are rising. Climate change is also altering the habitats of plants and animals. For instance, melting Arctic ice is reducing the hunting grounds of polar bears, and ocean acidification is destroying coral reefs, which are home to many different ocean creatures. The effects of a changing climate do not stop there. As the weather and the environment change, food production, water security, water quality, air quality, wildfire risk, and the spread of infectious diseases such as malaria are some of the many other factors that are affected.

A Changing Climate Threatens Humanity

Most experts believe that climate change poses a significant threat to humanity's well-being. This is because the climate is closely tied to people's most basic needs. "Climate change affects the food we eat, the air we breathe, the water we drink, and the places that provide us with shelter,"[7] explains the US

A wildfire burns near homes in Azusa, California. Worsening wildfires are just one of many climate change–related threats that are forcing people to adapt.

Environmental Protection Agency (EPA). A changing climate will impact humanity's ability to adequately meet these needs.

The 2023 annual report of the *Lancet* Countdown, a collaboration of international scientists and health practitioners, provides concrete examples of how the changing climate is already harming people. One thing that its 2023 report looked at was heat, which is the biggest cause of weather-related deaths. The *Lancet* Countdown found that global temperatures are higher than they have been in more than one hundred thousand years, increasing the risk of heat-related illness or death for many people. "Adults older than 65 years and infants younger than 1 year, for whom extreme heat can be particularly life-threatening, are now exposed to twice as many heatwave days as they would have experienced in 1986–2005,"

"Climate change affects the food we eat, the air we breathe, the water we drink, and the places that provide us with shelter."[7]

—US Environmental Protection Agency

it states. The report also mentions drought, another climate change–related event that causes significant harm: "The global land area affected by extreme drought increased from 18% in 1951–60 to 47% in 2013–22 . . . jeopardising water security, sanitation, and food production." On another front, the *Lancet* Countdown reports that 27 percent of cities surveyed were concerned about their health systems (hospitals, medicinal and equipment supplies, caregivers) being overwhelmed by the impacts of climate change. Overall, the authors conclude that the "rising risks of climate change are amplifying global health inequities and threatening the very foundations of human health."[8]

In addition to health, climate change threatens humanity's well-being in many other ways. For example, extreme weather events that kill people and destroy their homes and belongings are becoming more common. For example, in August 2024, unusually

Sea Level Rise

Climate change is causing sea levels to steadily rise, which will cause a variety of problems for humanity in the future. There are two main causes for sea level rise. First, as the climate warms, the world's ice sheets and glaciers are melting, which is adding more water to the seas. Second, as existing seawater warms, it expands, meaning the existing water will take up more space, further causing a rise in sea level. Experts are not exactly sure how much the sea will rise in the future, but they do expect it to be significant. According to the National Oceanic and Atmospheric Administration's most recent estimate, by 2100 the seas could be between 1.0 foot and 6.6 feet (0.3 m and 2.0 m) higher than they were in 2000.

Humanity will experience many different harms as seas rise. There will be more flooding from extreme weather events, such as hurricanes, and from regular tidal activity. Rising seas will also erode coastlines and cover low-lying areas of land. Another significant harm is saltwater intrusion, where saltwater will contaminate freshwater supplies. SeaLevelRise.org stresses, "There's a lot at risk from sea level rise and flooding. . . . [It] not only damages personal property, but threatens human health, emergency response time, city infrastructure, the economy, military readiness, and important habitats."

SeaLevelRise.org, "Overview." https://sealevelrise.org. Quoted in Will Oremus, "Google's AI Passed a Famous Test—and Showed How the Test Is Broken," *Washington Post*, June 17, 2022. www.washingtonpost.com.

heavy rain caused severe flooding in Bangladesh, with the United Nations Children's Fund reporting that people were stranded without food or water, and hundreds of thousands were seeking shelter. Around the world, significant numbers have been forced to permanently abandon their homes because of environmental conditions such as flooding, drought, heat, rising seas, or extreme storms. These people are often referred to as climate refugees or climate migrants, and climate change is expected to create millions of them over the coming years.

Climate Change Is Inevitable

Most climate change experts stress that humanity can mitigate, or lessen, climate change by reducing greenhouse gas emissions, which will limit the level of warming that occurs. However, it is widely recognized that even if emissions are reduced dramatically, the climate will continue to change for some time. This means that no matter what is done, a certain level of climate change is inevitable.

One reason experts say the climate will continue to change no matter what people do is that current greenhouse gas levels have triggered circular reactions that are difficult to stop and are accelerating the pace of change. For example, climate change causes Arctic sea ice and glaciers to melt, and as the ice melts, more areas of land and ocean are exposed. Whereas ice reflects the sun, the exposed areas of land and sea are dark and absorb rather than reflect sunlight. This causes the land and sea to warm faster and melt even more ice and snow, continuing a cycle of melting and warming. Another example is the way climate change causes increased heat and drought, which lead to more frequent wildfires. As trees burn, they release more carbon into the atmosphere; this causes the atmosphere to warm even more, which leads to an even greater chance of wildfires.

Some experts also worry that the buildup of emissions is not incremental, meaning the risks of climate change are not gradually increasing along with emissions. Instead, they talk about something called tipping points, where change could be sudden

Children in Kenya get water from holes in a dry riverbed. Drought causes significant hardship worldwide.

and catastrophic. Earth's climate system is complex and interconnected, and researchers worry that there are certain tipping points—or critical thresholds—that will lead to a significant and irreversible change. For instance, the Amazon is an important ecosystem that helps regulate rainfall and fresh water and keeps the climate stable. If too much of the Amazon rainforest is lost, then it could eventually reach a tipping point where it is unable to keep operating and could turn into an arid savannah. As it dies, it would release huge amounts of carbon, accelerating climate change even more. The loss of the Amazon would also significantly change weather and water supplies worldwide.

Adaptation Is Essential

As a result of the changing climate, humanity needs to take action to adapt. The Intergovernmental Panel on Climate Change (IPCC) is a body that was created by the United Nations (UN) to advance knowledge about climate change. According to the IPCC, "Climate change is a global threat to which all people and ecosys-

> **"Without effective adaptation, climate change has the potential to reverse the developmental gains in our world and push millions of people further into poverty."[9]**
>
> —Intergovernmental Panel on Climate Change

tems are vulnerable. Without effective adaptation, climate change has the potential to reverse the developmental gains in our world and push millions of people further into poverty. To avoid mounting losses, urgent accelerated action is required to adapt to climate change."[9] Adapting includes everything from individual actions like better insulating one's home to reduce the need to cool it in summer to countrywide efforts such as restricting new construction in areas that are vulnerable to wildfires or flooding.

Most experts recognize that the question is not *whether* adaptation will occur, but *how*. It is widely argued that delaying adaptation will simply make the process more difficult and expensive. "Investing in adaptation makes a lot more sense than waiting and trying to catch up later," explains the UN. "Protecting people now saves more lives and reduces risks moving forward. It makes financial sense too because the longer we wait, the more the costs will escalate."[10]

There are different types of adaptation. Some actions are taken in response to climate change effects that have already happened. For example, people who have lost their homes to flooding adapt by moving, or cities adapt to extreme temperatures by planting shade-providing trees to lessen summer heat. Adaptation can also anticipate changes that are coming. For instance, scientists are working to develop crops that will be more tolerant of extreme weather conditions, and cities can set up early warning systems in preparation for extreme weather events. Both of these adaptations can be beneficial, but some people believe that anticipatory adaptation is the most important because it can prevent future problems from even occurring—and save people a lot of money and trouble.

Vulnerable Groups

The negative effects of climate change are not distributed evenly around the world, so adaptation is even more critical for certain vulnerable populations. A variety of social, political, economic, and environmental factors make some people more vulnerable to the effects of climate change. For example, in the United States, low-income groups and communities of color are often more likely to live in older communities that are more vulnerable to heat or flooding caused by climate change; they also are more likely to have health problems that might be exacerbated by climate change–related hazards such as wildfire smoke.

Indigenous peoples are another group that often are more likely to feel the harms of climate change. In places such as the Amazon, Central America, and the Himalayas, Indigenous peoples heavily depend on natural resources and weather conditions for their survival. For example, Amazon tribes rely on the river and the rainforest for their food, water, shelter, clothing, and medicines. When that environment changes, their entire way of life is threatened. In some cases, Indigenous populations are even

Mentally Adapting to Climate Change

Not only will humanity need to adapt to the physical dangers posed by the changing climate, but a growing number of experts are realizing that mental adaptation will be required too. Research shows that a significant number of people are experiencing anxiety and mental distress in response to the threat of climate change. Clinical psychologist Sarah Lowe explains the concept of what many people are calling *climate anxiety*:

> Climate anxiety is fundamentally distress about climate change and its impacts on the landscape and human existence. That can manifest as intrusive thoughts or feelings of distress about future disasters or the long-term future of human existence and the world, including one's own descendants. There is a physiological component that would include heart racing and shortness of breath, and a behavioral component: when climate anxiety gets in the way of one's social relationships or functioning at work or school.

As climate change continues to alter life on the planet, psychologists believe that mental adaptation to these changes will be an important part of survival for humanity.

Quoted in Yale Sustainability, "Yale Experts Explain Climate Anxiety," March 13, 2023. https://sustainability.yale.edu.

forced to relocate. World Economic Forum writers report that climate change is displacing Indigenous communities at a rate seven times higher than that of the general global population. They give the example of the Kalash, who live in the mountains of Pakistan and are threatened by glacial flooding that has been amplified by climate change. They explain, "These floods pose serious risks, including soil erosion, species displacement and food insecurity." The risks are so serious that "the Kalash community, with a longstanding history in the region, now confronts an existential crisis, contemplating the necessity of relocation amidst mounting environmental challenges."[11]

Marginalized communities such as ethnic minorities, refugees, and low-income communities are also more vulnerable to the impacts of climate change. These groups are more likely to experience the harshest impacts and, with fewer resources at

A fisherman in the Amazon checks his net. Indigenous peoples rely on natural resources for survival and are vulnerable to the effects of climate change.

their disposal, will have more difficulty preparing for and dealing with the effects of climate change. On top of that, many of these communities are already vulnerable and may be treated unequally; climate change is likely to amplify these problems. For example, according to a 2021 report by the EPA, in the United States, African Americans are 40 percent more likely to live in areas that will have the greatest increases in deaths caused by extreme temperatures. The report also states that Latinos are 43 percent more likely to live in areas where they will lose work time as a result of extreme heat, and Native Americans and Alaska Natives are 48 percent more likely to live in areas that will flood due to sea level rise.

Where a person lives, how old they are, and their overall health can also affect their vulnerability to climate change. For example, people who live in floodplains or on coastlines are more likely to be affected by extreme weather. Certain populations are also more likely to experience harm from weather extremes. For example, children, the elderly, and people with certain health conditions are more vulnerable to extreme heat or to wildfire smoke. Adaptation is particularly important for these vulnerable groups because they are likely to be among the first to be harmed by climate change.

There are many compelling reasons for humanity to adapt to climate change. Climate change is a part of the future, and although certain vulnerable groups are likely to be harmed first, ultimately, everyone will experience long-term harm unless humanity takes action to adapt.

CHAPTER TWO

What Actions Can Humanity Take to Adapt?

Marinel Ubaldo was sixteen years old when she first realized the importance of adapting to climate change. After seeing a typhoon destroy her village in the Philippines, she realized that change was necessary. "I was really determined to do more because I didn't want to be vulnerable for the rest of my life," she says. "I didn't want other people to experience what we had experienced. . . . I didn't even know myself if I would survive during the typhoon."[12] Some of the ways Ubaldo has taken action to help her community include teaching adaptation strategies at youth camps, organizing mangrove plantings, spearheading community cleanups, recycling, participating in waste-segregation activities, and even writing a song with children and young people to teach about climate change.

As Ubaldo's story shows, there are many different things that humans can do to reduce the harmful effects of climate change now and to meet future challenges. Efforts to adapt include small actions like reducing water use and big projects like building million-dollar retaining walls to protect communities from sea level rise. Most experts agree it is key to do *something*, because climate change is happening, and failing to adapt is not an option.

Better Water Management

Some people argue that better management of water supplies should be one of humanity's first priorities for adapting to climate change. People cannot survive without water. They rely on it for drinking and sanitation as well as to grow crops and raise animals. However, water is also one of the resources most affected by climate change. In fact, the UN argues, "climate change is primarily a water crisis." It explains, "Extreme weather events are making water more scarce, more unpredictable, more polluted or all three. These impacts throughout the water cycle threaten sustainable development, biodiversity, and people's access to water and sanitation."[13] A significant number of people around the world already experience problems with water. For instance, as reported in the 2023 *United Nations World Water Development Report*, 26 percent of the world's people do not have access to safe drinking water, and

> **"Extreme weather events are making water more scarce, more unpredictable, more polluted or all three. These impacts throughout the water cycle threaten sustainable development, biodiversity, and people's access to water and sanitation."[13]**
>
> —United Nations

Young people march in the Philippines in 2021 to increase climate change awareness and promote adaptation efforts. Activism is just one way that people can help their communities prepare to meet the challenges that will come with climate change.

46 percent live without access to basic sanitation services such as toilets or water for handwashing. Problems like these are likely to become more pronounced as the climate changes, making water management a top priority.

There are many ways to improve water management, which will better equip communities to face the ways in which climate change is altering water supplies. Conserving, reusing, and recycling water are key to these efforts. Communities can embrace water-saving techniques such as watering crops more efficiently to avoid evaporation and waste and reducing waste in the home by using catchment water (rainwater caught in big basins) or recycling gray (used) water for lawns, gardens, or other secondary purposes. Communities can also build new infrastructure, such as water treatment plants and reservoirs, to help increase their resiliency in times of shortage. Education is also important for good water management. This means helping people understand the importance of managing water supplies properly and giving them the tools to do so.

Reducing Reliance on Air-Conditioning

Air-conditioning is one way that people cope with extreme heat. However, some experts argue that as heat waves become more widespread and longer lasting, communities must reduce their reliance on air-conditioning and find other ways to beat the heat. Climate change writer Daniel Cusick explains that air-conditioning is not an ideal solution for heat waves because air-conditioning is expensive, and many people cannot afford to run it even if they have it. In addition, if too many people use it at once (which is common during a heat wave), the power grid can become overwhelmed and result in power blackouts. He says, "Under such scenarios, houses and apartments equipped with air-conditioning can become death traps." Further, air-conditioning is energy intensive and can contribute to further climate change. Cusick explains there are other ways to prepare for future extreme heat. These include upgrading homes to make them cooler and planting trees and other greenery to cool urban areas.

Daniel Cusick, "How We Can Adapt to Live with Extreme Heat," *Scientific American*, July 21, 2023. www.scientificamerican.com.

Smart Growth

Smart growth is another way to adapt to a changing climate. Experts predict that in the future there are likely to be more droughts and heat waves, stronger storms, increased flooding, and a rise in sea levels. Smart growth means knowing which of these factors threaten a specific area and then planning future growth so the area will be more resilient to those threats. For instance, development can be discouraged in areas that are likely to experience increased sea level rise, storm surges, and flooding so fewer people will be present in these areas when disaster strikes. Developers can also plan for or leave areas of open space to help absorb flooding.

Smart growth also includes building homes and other structures in ways that are more climate resilient—such as being energy efficient or even energy self-generating (such as by using solar panels)—so people can make do if they lose power. The EPA also suggests designing buildings that can be moved. "Modular buildings can more easily be moved, renovated, and deconstructed as a community or tenant's needs change and as climate-related impacts change," it writes. "Strategies include using exposed mechanical fasteners, disentangling utilities from the structure, using moveable walls and ramps, using standard-sized modular building components and assemblies, and providing easy-to-understand information on construction drawings and documents."[14]

"Modular buildings can more easily be moved, renovated, and deconstructed as a community or tenant's needs change and as climate-related impacts change."[14]

—US Environmental Protection Agency

Another element of smart growth is upgrading stormwater systems and designing new ones that can handle the greater amounts of runoff and flooding that are likely to accompany more frequent and intense rainfall. Stormwater systems are collections of drains and pipes that help manage runoff when it rains. Experts are concerned that in the future, existing stormwater systems will not be able to handle the amount of runoff, which will cause a variety of problems, including erosion of the land, pollution of waterways, and even more flooding. To prevent these issues, developers can upgrade systems and also use more green infrastructure—such as permeable paving materials that absorb water—so that there is less runoff from paved surfaces.

Smart growth also includes considering how and where growth happens and managing it in areas that are particularly vulnerable to climate change impacts. For instance, smart growth strategies than can help reduce the impacts of wildfires include discouraging development in high-risk areas, increasing the space between buildings and forests, and using fire-resistant building materials.

Green Infrastructure to Reduce Urban Heat

Another type of smart growth is green infrastructure intended to minimize the effects of heat waves. This is particularly important in cities, which are often vulnerable to heat. The EPA explains that cities experience something called a "heat island effect":

> Heat islands are urbanized areas that experience higher temperatures than outlying areas. Structures such as buildings, roads, and other infrastructure absorb and re-emit the sun's heat more than natural landscapes such as forests and water bodies. Urban areas, where these structures are highly concentrated and greenery is limited, become "islands" of higher temperatures relative to outlying areas.[15]

Because of the heat island effect, compared to other areas, urban areas can have daytime temperatures that are 1°F to 7°F (0.6°C to 3.9°C) higher and nighttime temperatures that are 2°F to 5°F (1.1°C to 2.8°C) higher than nonurban areas.

There are many ways smart growth can help reduce the heat island effect. One is to plant more trees and other plants, which have a cooling effect. Not only do plants and trees provide shade, but they also act like a natural air conditioner because they absorb water from the soil and release it through their leaves, which

This photo shows a green roof on top of an apartment building in Monaco. Green roofs can help lower the temperature in a city.

cools the surrounding air. One innovative way to incorporate more greenery into cities is to build green roofs. A green roof is a garden or layer of plants on a rooftop. This can keep the roof and the air around it significantly cooler. According to the EPA, the temperature on a green roof can be 30°F to 40°F (17°C to 22°C) lower than a conventional roof and can help lower the overall temperature in a city by up to 5°F (2.8°C).

Another way to reduce city heat is to use new technology to create cool pavements and cool roofs. Traditional roofing and paving materials absorb significant amounts of heat, making cities hotter than rural areas. For instance, on hot days pavements can reach temperatures of up to 150°F (66°C). Cool roofs and pavements are made of materials that reflect heat back into the atmosphere rather than absorbing it. Most are also light colored because light colors generally reflect back the most heat. There are a variety of different coatings and materials used in cool roofs and pavements, and scientists are currently working on developing new technologies that will be even more effective at reflecting rather than absorbing heat.

Agricultural Adaptation

As the climate changes, crops, livestock, and other food sources are impacted by events such as flooding, droughts, and extreme weather. These events can cause losses and unpredictability in the food supply, and experts predict this will only worsen in the future. This means that agricultural adaptation is an important part of responding to climate change.

There are many ways to make the food supply more resilient to the effects of climate change. Researchers are currently working on developing new types of crops that are more resistant to heat and drought. Another solution is to reform the current agricultural system to make it healthier and less wasteful. For instance, farmers can try to improve the health of crop and pastureland so it will be more productive and more resilient to weather changes. The Natural Resources Defense Council explains how this works: "Grasses, legumes, and other plants protect exposed soil and prevent erosion, suppress weeds, sequester [capture and store] carbon from the atmosphere, and minimize flooding and nutrient runoff." Another solution is to reduce food waste. In the United States, for instance, it is estimated that 30 percent to 40 percent of the food supply goes to waste every year.

Natural Resources Defense Council, "Climate Change: Agriculture & Food." www.nrdc.org.

Preserve and Restore Ecosystems

Healthy ecosystems can also help with adaptation. They can absorb large amounts of carbon, thus helping to reduce warming, and can also help protect against extreme weather. For instance, coral reefs and coastal ecosystems can reduce the impacts of flooding by absorbing and slowing floodwater. Unfortunately, research shows that many of the ecosystems that can help with flood control have either been damaged or are in danger and thus need protection and restoration. Most experts insist that adaptation efforts should include preserving existing ecosystems and restoring those that have been damaged.

One specific ecosystem that can help with mitigation is mangroves. Mangroves are trees found along coastlines and in estuaries. Their distinctive-looking roots stretch down deep into the water. These trees can both absorb large amounts of carbon and help protect coastal areas from flooding and erosion. They also provide a habitat for fish and can thus help improve fish stocks that people rely on for food. According to the International Union for Conservation of Nature, approximately 15 percent of the coastlines in the world have mangroves on them, but half of these are at risk of collapse. Around the world, there are already a number of restoration projects where people are attempting to improve the health of these important ecosystems through efforts such as planting new seedlings and trying to improve existing coastal conditions to reverse declines experienced by plants already growing there.

Early Warning Systems

Another important adaptation effort is the development of early warning systems. Climate change is expected to cause more frequent and severe storms in the future. It is impossible to eliminate that fact, and people who live in certain areas will incur losses due to storms.

> **"Early warnings save lives and provide vast economic benefits. Just 24 hours' notice of an impending hazardous event can cut the ensuing damage by 30 per cent."[16]**
>
> —Petteri Taalas, secretary-general of the World Meteorological Organization

One way to adapt to this problem is to create systems that warn people when a storm is coming. An early warning means that people will have time to prepare for the storm and to evacuate if necessary. Some countries already use early warning systems. For example, in the United States, local television and radio stations broadcast weather warnings, and warnings are also sent to cellphones. According to Petteri Taalas, who is secretary-general of the organization, "Early warnings save lives and provide vast economic benefits. Just 24 hours' notice of an impending hazardous event can cut the ensuing damage by 30 per cent."[16] However, according to a report by the World Meteorological Organization, at least a third of the world's people are not covered by early warning systems.

Early warning systems can be improved by increasing the collection and analysis of weather and climate data to better identify risks. Systems can also be developed to better communicate

In India, an early warning system task force member warns community members of an impending flood. Early warning systems can give people time to prepare and to evacuate if necessary.

warnings to those who will be affected. The Maldives is doing both of these. As one of the lowest-lying countries in the world, this island nation often experiences flooding from storms. It is working to improve its early warning systems so people will be aware of an impending disaster. This effort involves using technology to improve data collection and analysis and creating reliable communication channels that can be used to reach even those who live in remote areas.

Monitoring and Evaluation

Monitoring and evaluation are also an important climate change adaptation strategy. As the US Department of Agriculture (USDA) explains, "Climate adaptation is the process of adjusting to avoid the expected or actual consequences of climate change." Ongoing monitoring and evaluation entail collecting a lot of data about exactly how the climate is changing, various adaptation efforts that are being implemented, and the effects of these. After that, the data is analyzed to provide a solid understanding of the climate change problems that need to be addressed and which adaptation efforts might be successful. The USDA says, "Climate adaptation at USDA is an iterative process of assessment, planning, implementation, and monitoring and evaluation."[17]

Most experts advise that adaptation will be a continually changing process that involves constant monitoring and evaluation. As researchers gain a better understanding of how current adaptation efforts are working, adaptation strategies can be adjusted accordingly. In a recent report, the IPCC stresses that there are still a lot of things people do not understand about adaptation. It explains, "For example, the extent to which adaptation actions are reducing climate risk, and for whom, is not always clear. Another important question is whether adaptation actions may have unintended consequences or side effects, causing more harm than good."[18] Monitoring and evaluation can help answer some of these questions.

Climate change will be a part of humanity's future. However, from the individual to the government level, there are many ways people and cities can adapt to a future that will be significantly different. As the World Wildlife Fund stresses, "A warming climate is changing our world. While we can't turn back time, we can make life on Earth as resilient to change as possible."[19]

CHAPTER THREE

Why Is Adaptation Challenging?

Like almost every other part of the world, Scotland is experiencing significant climate-related changes. In the future, its residents can expect both warmer and wetter winters, with more frequent and extreme weather events. In Glasgow, the country's largest city, a number of projects have been initiated to help residents adapt. For example, some of the city's old buildings—built over a hundred years ago—are being renovated so residents can live more comfortably and with more energy efficiency. However, the process has not been without challenges. Journalist Calum Watson explains that renovating the old structures can cause unintended problems. "Making an old building airtight creates new problems with condensation and mould, so mechanical ventilation and moisture reduction are also part of the work," he says. To solve those problems, developers had to create suitcase-sized ventilation units that they installed in bathroom ceilings to take out the moist air. The cost of the retrofit was substantial. Watson asks a question on many people's minds when it comes to climate change adaptation efforts: "Who will pay?"[20]

"Climate change is one of the most complex issues facing us today. It involves many dimensions—science, economics, society, politics, and moral and ethical questions."[21]

—National Aeronautics and Space Administration

Adapting to climate change is not easy. NASA calls climate change "one of the most complex issues facing us today. It involves many dimensions—science, economics, society, politics, and moral and ethical questions."[21] Successful adaptation may require knowledge, money, coordination, and desire, among other things, which makes it multifaceted and thus challenging.

Finances

One of the biggest challenges to adaptation is finding the money to pay for solutions. There are many potential ways to adapt, but executing them is costly. According to the 2023 *Adaptation Gap Report* of the United Nations Environment Programme (UNEP), finance needs for adaptation are significant, and the world is not even close to having the necessary funds. The organization discusses the adaptation finance gap, which is defined as the difference between what is needed and what is actually being provided. It states, "The adaptation finance gap is widening and now stands at between US$194 billion and US$366 billion per year. Adaptation finance needs are 10–18 times as great as current international public adaptation finance flows."[22]

A person replaces old windows in a house to combat heat.

In many cases, poor and developing countries are the most vulnerable to climate change and thus most in need of adaptation. However, these countries are typically the ones least likely to have the resources to pay for adaptation strategies. According to the *Adaptation Gap Report*, the adaptation costs for developing countries will be somewhere between $215 billion and $387 billion per year for the decade of the 2020s, which is significantly more than previously estimated. Not only do developing countries not have this money, but the report also shows that in recent years, they are actually receiving less international aid for adaptation efforts. "This is a hugely worrying deceleration," says UNEP's executive director, Inger Andersen. "Finding new ways to deliver finance for adaptation action is essential."[23]

Lack of Political Commitment

Although individual action is important, successful adaptation requires government action. Governments have the power and resources to address problems of the size, scope, and scale of climate change. They can engage and educate the population, provide funding, and lead implementation of adaptation policies. Robert Stavins, a professor of energy and economic development at the Harvard Kennedy School of Government, talks about the role of government in helping to promote renewable energy. "Individual action is not going to be sufficient in 10 or even 20 years," he says. "You need government policies to create incentives for industry and individuals."[24]

David G. Victor and Veerabhadran Ramanathan are climate experts with the Scripps Institution of Oceanography in San Diego. They explain that strong government leadership is a key element in climate adaptation because it can coordinate scattered efforts into a cohesive strategy. They state,

> Adaptation to the consequences of global warming doesn't come just from singular activities, like flipping a switch; it's processes that will affect all of society and can

> easily go awry. Similarly, a serious resilience strategy can't be piecemeal: It involves power grids and other infrastructure that must be managed at a large scale, and every locality needs to learn from ideas that get tested around the country and world. That's why we need a national approach that assesses how local efforts fit together, how much money to spend on each component and which policies actually work.[25]

Around the world, many governments are talking about climate change adaptation, making policies, and setting goals, but some think they are not doing much to actually enact change. Three former UN climate chiefs—Christiana Figueres, Yvo de Boer, and Michael Zammit Cutajar—argue that, worldwide, governments have failed to act. They call on the world's governments to stop making excuses and take action. "The United Nations Framework Convention on Climate Change was adopted 30 years ago," they say. "In our time leading its secretariat [administration], we have witnessed commitments and pledges that have not been fully honoured. While developed countries accepted the convention's

Too Much Focus on Stopping Emissions

The idea of adaptation as a necessary response to climate change has only recently gained widespread public acceptance. For many years, the focus was more on reducing emissions—a strategy known as mitigation—to stop climate change, and adaptation was widely seen as the wrong thing to focus on. Journalist Madeline Ostrander explains: "Some climate experts felt that any talk about adaptation distracted from the work of keeping pollution out of the atmosphere: it sounded less like a coping mechanism and more like giving up."

Many experts argue that the early focus on mitigation made adaptation efforts more challenging because it delayed action, ultimately making adaptation more difficult and expensive. Ostrander says, "If adaptation and mitigation experts had come together, perhaps they would have . . . overcome more obstacles sooner."

Madeline Ostrander, "Why We Can No Longer Afford to Ignore the Case for Climate Adaptation," *MIT Technology Review*, August 17, 2022. www.technologyreview.com.

principle of equity and thus their responsibility to lead climate action, their performance has been disappointing."[26]

Lack of Information

Another challenge to adaptation is a lack of information. To effectively adapt to climate change, society needs accurate information about what is happening—for instance, how quickly oceans are rising or how much temperatures are changing each year. Most experts say that at present, there are not enough systems to monitor and analyze climate change data. This means it is difficult for communities and governments to make effective adaptation plans. The IPCC has noted that large, critical gaps remain in our understanding. "The extent to which adaptation actions are reducing climate risk, and for whom, is not always clear," it says. "Another important question is whether adaptation actions may have unintended consequences or side effects, causing more harm than good (this is called maladaptation)."[27] For example, a seawall might be built to help a community protect against sea level rise, but this effort can cause harm if it is built in a way that, say, harms the coastal ecosystem or causes more erosion.

"The United Nations Framework Convention on Climate Change was adopted 30 years ago. In our time leading its secretariat [administration], we have witnessed commitments and pledges that have not been fully honoured."[26]

—Christiana Figueres, Yvo de Boer, and Michael Zammit Cutajar, former UN climate chiefs

The need for information is an ongoing challenge because climate change and its harms are an ever-evolving situation. The IPCC explains, "In a warming world, measures that are effective now in one place might not work in 20 years, or in other places, which is why the monitoring and evaluation of the implemented actions are so important. Adaptation strategies might have to be revised constantly and those revisions will be most efficient if they are fact- and data-driven."[28] Unfortunately, only a few countries currently have effective systems with which to do this.

This photo shows world leaders at a 2022 climate summit in Egypt. While there is a lot of talk about climate change adaptation, critics say that most governments are not doing enough to enact change.

No Sense of Urgency

In many cases, adaptation is not prioritized because some people simply do not feel a sense of urgency about problems related to climate change. According to a 2023 Pew Research Center report, three in ten people—30 percent—believe that action on climate change is not important or should not be taken. Compared to other priorities, such as the economy and health care, people ranked climate change relatively low: seventeenth out of twenty-one national issues, in relation to urgency. A March 2024 Gallup poll showed that 55 percent of people do not believe that climate change will be a serious threat in their lifetime. Only 59 percent said they thought the effects of global warming had already begun.

> "In a warming world, measures that are effective now in one place might not work in 20 years, or in other places, which is why the monitoring and evaluation of the implemented actions are so important."[28]
>
> —Intergovernmental Panel on Climate Change

One reason for this complacency is that many people have not yet personally experienced the harms of climate change; thus, it

Going with the Flow

One challenge that frustrates efforts to adapt to climate change is the fact that many people have a tendency to do nothing, even though they know that climate change is a threat and understand that adaptation will be required. "When it comes to climate change, most of us are full of good intentions," writes Eoin Redahan for the *Society of Chemical Industry Blog*. "We want to do the right thing but when change becomes too difficult or inconvenient, people (like me) lapse into old habits."

Such behavior is confirmed by Toby Park, who works at the Behavioural Insights Team, a global organization that uses knowledge about human behavior to drive positive change. He explains that people tend to follow whatever the majority is doing. "We are like swimmers in a stream," he says. "We have the opportunity to swim in one direction or another but we are in a stream that has a current." When it comes to issues as large and multifaceted as climate change, it can be difficult to get people to break out of that current.

Quoted in Eoin Redahan, "Why Are We Ignoring Climate Change?," *Society of Chemical Industry Blog*, March 2, 2022. www.soci.org.

simply does not feel like a critical issue to them. Cognitive scientist Art Markman explains that people are hardwired to appreciate urgent threats like a vicious dog growling at them, but they have more trouble acting on threats that seem farther away or bigger than the current moment, such as climate change often does. In addition, Markman says, the benefits of adapting to climate change may not be felt until the future, and it is human nature to focus more on shorter-term actions that appear to have more tangible results. "People don't save enough money for retirement, preferring to spend money now rather than having it in their old age," says Markman of human tendencies. "People overeat in the present, despite the problems that obesity can cause in the future." People can have the same reaction to climate change: "Ignoring climate change in the short term has benefits both to individuals and to organizations. Individuals do not have to make changes in the cars they drive, the products they buy, or the homes they live in."[29]

The Pew Research Center uncovered other reasons for the general lack of urgency related to climate change when it conducted in-depth interviews with survey participants who described climate action as a low priority. A common reason was the belief that current warming is simply part of a natural cycle. As one person put it, "I think that there's climate change but I think this planet is, I don't know, how many millions if not billions of years old and that's just probably a cycle that it goes through. I think humans probably have a very, very minor part of it but it is also just things out of our control."[30] Another common opinion was that climate change is not urgent enough to pass laws that restrict individual freedoms. "Don't ban gas combustion vehicles. Don't ban gas stoves," said one respondent. "Give people the information. Let them decide what they want to do. But when you start to force things upon people, that's when people become skeptical. It's like, why are they forcing something on to us? Why are they changing laws?"[31]

Adaptation Is Not Always Possible

Another issue stems from the fact that not all climate change–related challenges can be solved by adaptation. The IPCC stresses that there are limits to adaptation: "The availability of adaptation options is constrained by limitations faced by the natural world and people, especially at higher degrees of warming." For example, in some cases, adaptation may be physically impossible. The IPCC gives the example of small islands that are threatened by rising seas and are losing both land and freshwater supplies. In cases such as these, where the islands are disappearing, the IPCC says that "inhabitants may have no other option than to abandon their homes."[32]

However, although adaptation is not always the answer, most experts agree that it is a significant part of the solution. Humanity faces a number of challenges in its attempts to adapt, but people have also managed to come up with many innovative strategies and are likely to continue to do so in the future.

How Has Humanity Been Successful?

Bangladesh is a low-lying and densely populated country that is extremely vulnerable to the effects of climate change. It often experiences devastating cyclones and flooding that displace thousands of people. However, Bangladesh is also an example of success when it comes to climate change adaptation. It was one of the first countries to develop a national action plan to reduce the harms of climate change, which considered food security, disaster management, infrastructure, and sustainable development. The plan's actions include building hundreds of cyclone shelters and keeping emergency medical teams on standby so they are ready to help in an emergency. Although Bangladesh is still frequently hit by cyclones, the World Bank Group reports that since 1970, the country has drastically reduced cyclone-related deaths. Overall, the World Bank Group says that Bangladesh "is recognized as a global leader in climate change adaptation and disaster preparedness."[33]

Bangladesh is just one example of how, even in the face of substantial odds, it is possible to take action to reduce the harms from climate change. Although the challenges are significant, all over the world individuals, communities, and governments have experienced successes in their efforts to adapt.

Increased Awareness

One of the biggest successes in climate change adaptation has simply been getting people, governments, and communities to be more aware of climate change–related

> **"[Bangladesh] is recognized as a global leader in climate change adaptation and disaster preparedness."[33]**
>
> —World Bank Group

threats and the urgent need to adapt. Just ten years ago, many people believed that climate change was not really happening, let alone an issue that required behavioral change. Since then, research shows that there has been significant increases in public awareness of climate change. When people are aware, they are more likely to take part in and support adaptation measures.

Increased awareness is revealed in many public surveys. For example, the 2024 Peoples' Climate Vote, a survey carried out by the UNDP and the University of Oxford, revealed widespread awareness of climate change and the necessity of adaptation among people in seventy-seven countries. One-third (33 percent) of those surveyed said that they think about climate change every day, and 69 percent said that many of their big life decisions, such as where to live and what to buy, are impacted by climate change. Seventy-nine percent said that richer countries should help poorer countries with adaptation efforts.

This photo shows people huddled in a cyclone shelter in Bangladesh. The country has built shelters and taken many other actions to adapt to storms that are becoming more frequent and severe as the climate changes.

Adapting to Extreme Heat in the United States

In recent years, the United States has seen an increase in the number and severity of heat waves as well as an increase in the number of people dying from these events. To address the growing threat from extreme heat, both local and national governments have taken many different actions that will help them be better prepared for future heat waves.

For example, the national government has created a portal called the National Integrated Heat Health Information System, which includes many detailed maps of heat-related threats, including a map of urban heat islands and a heat tracker that contains both historical data and forecasts for the future. This portal aims to help both the public and policy makers understand where the greatest heat threats are so they can develop strategies to face them. These strategies will vary by location but might include things like planting more trees to reduce heat in the future or preparing resources in order to deal with upcoming heat waves.

On the local level, many cities have created the new position of heat officer, who is charged with helping the city more effectively deal with extreme heat–related issues and educating the public about this risk.

National and International Adaptation Plans

As global awareness of the problem has increased, so have large-scale, coordinated adaptation efforts. The UNFCCC has encouraged this by creating the National Adaptation Plan (NAP). This is a way for countries to officially plan for adaptation and receive UN funding to help implement their plans. Making a plan involves using science to identify pressing challenges related to climate change and then creating a specific strategy to meet them. The UN reported that as of 2024, more than 140 countries have submitted NAPs. The United States has a number of its own adaptation plans. For instance, under the Federal Sustainability Plan, it will continually assess vulnerabilities and risks and modernize policies and infrastructure in response.

Along with many other countries, the United States was a signatory to the Paris Agreement, which is a legally binding international climate change treaty that includes adaptation goals. The Paris Agreement went into effect in 2016 and has been adopted by 195 parties. One component of it is the Global Goal on Adaptation (GGA), which focuses on coordinating adaptation efforts at a global level. World Resources Institute explains that although much remains to be done, member countries have managed to make important progress. For instance, in 2023, they agreed on an overall framework for the GGA, something that took eight years to achieve. The organization explains that this is an important step in global adaptation plans: "This framework provides a strong foundation, laying out broad global adaptation goals and key areas for action."[34] The agreement on a framework is seen as significant because so many countries—each with their own unique goals and opinions—are involved in the GGA, and it has been challenging for them to agree on anything.

Managing Water

Better water management is a key part of climate change adaptation. Water, which is crucial to life, is one of the resources most affected by climate change. One success story comes from Bagamoyo, Tanzania, where drought, rising sea levels, and inconsistent rainfall have made wells salty. In the past, students at one Tanzanian school had to choose between not drinking water all day or getting sick from salty well water. "We were sometimes not drinking water from morning until evening," says student Ismat Hassan. "Sometimes I'd have pain in my head and my body would lose energy."[35] Hassan got stomach ulcers after drinking the well water, and she developed a bacterial infection called typhoid after drinking dirty water from watering holes nearby. To solve the problem, Hassan's school constructed a rainwater harvesting system, collecting water in rooftop gutters and storing it in large tanks that hold 38,833 gallons (147,000 L) of water. Engineer Dickson Watson explains, "These tanks will help them store water on rainy days so that they can use that water when the rain goes away."[36]

"We were sometimes not drinking water from morning until evening. . . . Sometimes I'd have pain in my head and my body would lose energy."[35]

—Ismat Hassan, student

Rainwater harvest systems, like this one in Rwanda, Africa, are one way to better manage water supplies.

People in Darfur, a region of Sudan, have also taken action to better manage their water supplies. In this area, rainfall has steadily decreased in recent years, and water is scarce. This is making it increasingly difficult for the farmers who live there to support themselves. Their solution has been to create a better water management system that includes canals and weirs (tiny dams) to control water supplies and distribute them more efficiently and fairly. UNEP details some of the benefits of the project: "First, increased crop yield. In some cases, there has been a tripling of the yields for sorghum and millet—the staple food of the region—in places touched by the project. Second, an increase in income for the farmers. Seven of 10 farmers surveyed say that their income from agriculture has increased. And they credit this directly to the project."[37]

Fighting Sea Level Rise

Another example of successful adaptation comes from the small Pacific island state of Tuvalu. This tiny group of islands is at such a low elevation that experts have estimated that by 2050 half of its capital city will be flooded. Rather than accepting that fate, residents have fought to reclaim their home. "It's true climate change is affecting us, but we want to stay," says resident Fenuatapo Mesako. "We don't want to be Tuvaluans in another country. We want to be Tuvaluans in Tuvalu."[38] In 2023, Tuvalu completed part of an ambitious project designed to protect its main island, Funafuti, from the rising ocean through 2100. Under this plan, dredging was used to reclaim land. An area of higher ground was created that is expected to remain beyond the reach of storm waves and above sea level rise through at least 2100. Tuvalu plans to carry out similar efforts on some of its other islands.

A different island nation, Fiji, has employed the tactic of relocation to adapt to the challenge of rising sea levels. Fiji is made up of more than three hundred islands located in the South Pacific. Like Tuvalu, it has many low-lying areas that, as the sea rises, have experienced flooding, shoreline erosion, and saltwater intrusion, which is the contamination of freshwater supplies by saltwater. Consider the situation on Serua Island, one of many areas in Fiji that is facing growing intrusion from the sea. "Boats moor next to living rooms on Fiji's Serua Island, where water breaches the seawall at high tide, flooding into the village," write journalists Loren Elliot and Kristy Needham. "Planks of wood stretch between some homes, forming a makeshift walkway as saltwater inundates gardens."[39]

In response to the continually deteriorating quality of life in some areas, the country has made a plan to relocate almost fifty villages, establishing a fund to help. Six villages have already been relocated. Sera Naidrua, a resident of Vunidogoloa, was among the first to be relocated. "It was a good decision relocating here," she says of the village's new location. "We were fearing for our lives because of cyclones, inundation of waves in the village. . . . We feel safer."[40]

Restoring Ecosystems

Restoring ecosystems is another way communities are adapting to climate change. Ecosystems can be a valuable tool in adaptation.

Individual Adaptation Efforts

Some research shows that there has been a significant increase in adaptation efforts by individuals. In one study, which was published in *Nature Climate Change* on October 12, 2023, researchers from twelve different countries examined more than fourteen hundred studies on human adaptation to climate change. They found that individuals are a driving force of climate change adaptation—but in a different way than governments. Individuals are taking tangible actions, including moving away from areas with a higher flood risk, changing their work schedules to avoid extreme heat, and planting crops that are more resilient to climate change. "The evidence suggests that individuals and households are the primary adaptation actors—the ones actually implementing ways to adapt to the changes wrought by climate change," says study coauthor Christine Kirchhoff. "Geographically, in higher income countries, the government may begin to take the lead in planning or financing, but individuals are the ones taking action on the ground."

Quoted in Ashley WennersHerron, "Adapting to Climate Change: Individuals Take Action While Governments Plan," Pennsylvania State University, October 24, 2023. www.psu.edu.

For example, the UNDP explains that healthy wetlands help improve water quality and regulate the movement of water, making communities more resilient to both drought and flooding. It says, "Wetlands can provide support in absorbing excess water from intense rains and help regulate water flow through natural channels ensuring access during extended dry periods. The natural filtration capacity of wetlands can also enhance water quality."[41]

"Wetlands can provide support in absorbing excess water from intense rains and help regulate water flow through natural channels ensuring access during extended dry periods."[41]

—United Nations Development Programme

Raquel Castillo Puentes lives with her husband and daughter on a plot of land in Colombia's wetlands, an area known as La Mojana. With the support of a restoration program supported by Colombia's Adaptation Fund and its Ministry of Environment, she has started a nursery on her land, which has tens of thousands of seedlings in it that will eventually be planted in the community to help restore the wetlands. The UNDP says, "The Mojana communities have already restored 305 hectares (about 3 square kilometers [754 acres or 1.2 sq. mi]). Raquel alone has planted 1,124 trees on 1.2 hectares [3 acres]."[42]

People in the African nation of Gambia are also restoring their ecosystem so they can better adapt to climate change. Their efforts focus on restoring forests to make communities less vulnerable to flooding. Healthy forests protect against erosion and reduce damage. In addition, Gambians are restoring coastal mangrove forests that can also reduce flooding because they act as a buffer between the ocean and the land. UNEP, which is helping to fund these efforts, estimates that more than forty-six thousand households will benefit from these projects.

Using Climate Data

Yet another example of successful climate change adaptation involves collecting and analyzing climate data to make communities more resilient to climate change–related disasters. One place where data collection has increased is Pakistan, which is experiencing significant harm as a result of climate change. Pakistan

Some parts of Pakistan experienced devastating floods in 2022, made worse because many people were not properly prepared. This 2022 photo shows flood-damaged buildings in northwest Pakistan.

contains thousands of glaciers, which are an important source of freshwater for its citizens. However, as average temperatures rise and heat waves become more common, these glaciers are melting, which increases the risk of landslides and flooding. Glacial flooding has resulted in the creation of hundreds of lakes that are dammed with ice. If an ice dam breaks, catastrophic flooding can destroy mountain communities.

Muhammad Rasheed Mughal, who lives in Domail Pine, Pakistan, talks about the devastating flooding his village experienced in 2022. "Last year's flood swept away bridges, residential houses, land and everything," he says. "If the glaciers burst again this year and there is a flood, the remaining village will be washed away."[43] It is estimated that in 2022, more than seventeen hundred people died in Pakistan due to flooding.

One reason this flooding is so devastating is that people are not prepared for it. So, researchers are trying to collect more weather data, use technology to monitor and forecast weather more accurately, and warn at-risk communities more quickly in case of a flood or other dangerous event. The UNDP explains, "The project is installing 50 automatic weather stations in 24 valleys, as well as more than 400 water depth gauges, river discharge sensors, rain gauges, warning posts, and an alarm system. The data, which will be available in real time to anyone through the Meteorological Department's website, will help safeguard communities from potential glacial floods."[44] It says that this will significantly increase the number of people who will be able to receive early warning messages.

Around the world, adaptation efforts are widely varied, and include a range of different strategies and project sizes. While not every effort is successful, overall, humanity has seen a lot of success in its efforts to adapt to climate change, and around the world people continue to come up with new and innovative strategies for dealing with this threat.

What Actions Need to Be Taken in the Future?

In 2024, the European Environment Agency (EEA) published the *European Climate Risk Assessment*, a report intended to prioritize adaptation efforts in the European Union (EU). The EU has already taken many actions to make its member countries more resilient to climate change; in fact, many people consider the EU to be a leader in this field. However, according to this report, it needs to do a lot more—and must do so quickly. "Europe is the fastest warming continent in the world, and climate risks are threatening its energy and food security, ecosystems, infrastructure, water resources, financial stability, and people's health," warns the EEA. "Many of these risks have already reached critical levels and could become catastrophic without urgent and decisive action."[45]

The EU is not the only place where more action is needed. Around the world, people have done many things—both on individual and countrywide levels—to adapt to climate change. However, despite these efforts, many of them successful, it is widely recognized that all of humanity needs to do more if it wants to adapt to climate change.

Reduce Emissions

Reducing greenhouse gas emissions to slow the rate of climate change is a crucial step. Most experts agree that although the world has made progress in reducing emissions, it has not done enough. Under the Paris Agreement,

Successful adaptation must include a reduction of greenhouse gas emissions. Renewable energy sources such as these wind turbines in the Netherlands are one way to reduce emissions.

countries have agreed that they will try to limit warming to 2.7°F (1.5°C) above preindustrial levels. In the 2023 *Lancet* Countdown report on climate change, the authors warn that the world is not on track to meet this goal of 2.7°F (1.5°C). They state, "Data this year show a world that is often moving in the wrong direction. . . . Although countries committed to pursuing 'efforts to limit the temperature increase to 1.5°C above pre-industrial levels' in the 2015 Paris Agreement, GHG [greenhouse gas] emissions reached record levels in 2021, and again in 2022." The authors state that under current policies, the global temperature is likely to increase 4.9°F (2.7°C) by 2100, which they call "potentially catastrophic."[46] Adaptation expert Lara Hansen is one of many experts who stress that if humanity does not reduce emissions significantly, climate change will be so severe that people will not be able to adapt to it. She says, "Unchecked, climate change is unadaptable—like, we will so fundamentally change the landscape of the planet that it would be impossible."[47]

When it comes to reducing emissions, the United States has a major part to play because it is one of the world's biggest emitters of greenhouse gases. According to the Emissions Database for Global Atmospheric Research, in 2023 the world's largest emitters were China, the United States, the European Union, Russia, and Brazil, together accounting for 62.7 percent of the global total. In the United States, the majority of emissions come from the burning of fossil fuels for transportation and power, so one of the most effective ways to reduce emissions is to decrease the use of fossil fuels and increase the use of renewable fuel sources. Overall, the country is using more renewables and working to update its power grids and transportation networks to be compatible with these sources. However, most experts agree that much more progress is needed. For example, according to the US Energy Information Administration, in 2024 only about 16 percent of cars being purchased in the United States were electric vehicles or hybrids, meaning that 84 percent were still fossil fuel–burning cars.

Do More to Help Vulnerable Communities

Another area in which most researchers agree the world is not making enough progress is in helping vulnerable communities. Critics argue that vulnerable communities often are more likely to be harmed by climate change, but many adaptation efforts ignore or exclude these communities. The World Health Organization is one of many groups that stress that adaptation efforts need to include more actions to help the vulnerable. It says, "While no one is safe from these risks, the people whose health is being harmed first and worst by the climate crisis are the people who contribute least to its causes, and who are least able to protect themselves and their families against it: people in low-income and disadvantaged countries and communities."[48]

One way to help vulnerable communities is to include them in adaptation assessment and planning efforts to gain a better understanding of their unique needs. World Resources Institute writers Mathilde Bouyé and David Waskow insist, "Fair climate

Learn from the Past

As humanity tries to adapt to climate change, it can learn a lot from history, which is full of examples of communities adapting to climate change. By looking at these examples, people today might discover some innovative solutions.

In an article about history and climate change adaptation, Joe Wegener of the Boston Consulting Group and Chitresh Saraswat of the World Economic Forum provide one example. They state, "In present-day Spain, for example, farmers and researchers are excavating acequias, a network of irrigation canals built by the Moors during the Middle Ages. For centuries, the network distributed water from the Alpujarra Mountains across Andalusia, one of Europe's driest regions. Today, the canals are being revived as critical irrigation channels, helping Spain's farmers adapt to hotter and drier growing seasons." Researchers hope that by learning from examples like this, humanity can find new and creative ideas for adaptation.

Joe Wegener and Chitresh Saraswat, "What History Can Teach Us About Climate Adaptation," World Economic Forum, September 19, 2023. www.weforum.org.

actions largely rest on including the voices of disadvantaged groups in decision-making and, whenever possible, letting them make choices on measures that affect their lives." They point out that this might take some creativity. For example, they discuss the case of some African countries where widespread illiteracy can be an obstacle to involvement; to overcome this, policy makers have used citizens' deliberation processes, bringing groups of people together to talk about the issues. They state, "In Senegal, Ghana and Uganda, for example, citizens' deliberation processes have provided briefing materials to residents, enabling communities with high illiteracy rates to design robust proposals for resident relocation after flooding, as well as more sustainable use of natural resources."[49]

More Research and Education

There is still a lot that people do not know about climate change and how to respond to it, and most experts insist this needs to change. One way to increase understanding is to make information about climate change and adaptation more widely accessible. The UNDP explains how Bosnia and Herzegovina has been making this happen. It says that this country often experiences both drought and flooding, which affect many of the services that citizens depend on, such as water, energy, and agriculture. A few years ago, Bosnia and Herzegovina created an environmental informational system. The UNDP explains that with this system, Bosnia and Herzegovina can "gather, organize and update relevant data and make it accessible to all stakeholders engaged in decision-making."[50] In addition, the agency says that people at all levels of the country's government have been trained to use the system. With the information being collected, and the ability to analyze it, experts have helped Bosnia and Herzegovina better plan future adaptation efforts. For instance, the country has decided to prioritize water management because the data reveals a high likelihood of heavy precipitation and flooding in the future.

Another way to better educate communities about climate change and adaptation is to include it in school curricula. This is already happening in some places. For example, in 2020 New Jersey became the first US state to require climate change education in schools. The New Jersey Department of Environmental Protection explains, "The young people sitting in classrooms today will be the leaders in the continuing battle against the climate crisis. We must prepare them to be climate literate, with comprehensive and accurate knowledge of the environment around them."[51]

"The young people sitting in classrooms today will be the leaders in the continuing battle against the climate crisis. We must prepare them to be climate literate."[51]

—New Jersey Department of Environmental Protection

Proponents of climate change education believe that such programs should be expanded, and even the youngest children should benefit from them. New York City elementary teacher Kristy Neumeister says, "If they start this in kindergarten with those basic concepts, then by the time students come to third grade, there will be so much

An electric car charges in a garage in Washington, DC. Only a small percentage of the cars sold in the United States are electric; most still run on fossil fuels.

more knowledge." She adds, "They would become kind of little experts, and it would become a part of their lifestyle, and their parents would know about it, too."[52]

Proactive Adaptation

Many types of climate change adaptation are occurring in response to problems that communities are already facing, but experts argue that people also need to anticipate potential future problems and take action before those problems occur. An example of this comes from the city of Boston after Hurricane Sandy struck its neighbor, New York City, in 2012 and caused billions of dollars in damage. The U.S. Climate Resilience Toolkit website explains: "Boston city leaders—mindful of the toll—determined to take action before a similar extreme weather crisis struck their metropolis."[53] The city came up with an initiative called Climate Ready Boston that identified ways that Boston is vulnerable to climate change, and it is taking actions to reduce these vulnerabilities. For example, the plan identified coastal areas of Boston that are at risk of flooding due to climate change, and the city is now in the midst of efforts to protect those areas. One completed project is Langone Park in the North End, where athletic fields were raised above the flood zone and a seawall was constructed for further protection.

Most experts believe that proactive efforts have many benefits. By trying to anticipate future problems and creating solutions for them now, communities may be able to lessen future damage and loss of life from climate change–related events such as storms. In many cases, proactive adaptation measures are much cheaper than rebuilding a community after it has already been harmed by climate change.

Increase Financing for Adaptation

In addition to research and education, adapting to climate change will require a lot of money. Although worldwide investment has increased significantly in recent years, most experts agree that nowhere near enough is being spent. They argue that adaptation finance must increase substantially. In fact, the UN argues that it should be doubled. The bulk of this money, it insists, should come from wealthier countries that have played a significant role in causing the problem. "Justice demands that those who have contributed more to the problem assume a greater responsibility for solving it," the UN says. Achieving justice "depends on wealthier nations providing finance to countries with more limited means so they can keep up with enormous financial burdens as climate change accelerates."[54]

"Justice . . . depends on wealthier nations providing finance to countries with more limited means so they can keep up with enormous financial burdens as climate change accelerates."[54]

—United Nations

Indigenous Communities Want to Be More Involved

Governments around the world meet and make plans about climate change adaptation, but many Indigenous communities argue that they have been left out of these efforts. For instance, in 2023 world leaders met at a climate summit in Dubai, where they discussed the need for action to keep global warming to less than 2.7°F (1.5°C) above preindustrial levels, a target that was set in 2015. A number of Indigenous activists were at the summit, where they argued that their communities have been more heavily affected by climate change and so should have a greater voice in future plans. "We already live the 1.5 degree Celsius of the climate change impact," said Indigenous activist Hindou Oumarou Ibrahim from Chad. According to activists like Ibrahim, not only are Indigenous people often the most affected by climate change, but they also have the potential to be part of the solution because of their depth of knowledge about biodiversity and caring for the land.

Quoted in Jenny Gross, "Indigenous Delegates Say They're Already Living with Devastating Consequences of Climate Change," *New York Times*, December 1, 2023. www.nytimes.com.

However, not all climate change adaptation strategies are astronomically expensive. Consider early warning systems that warn of an impending disaster, often by mobile phone alert. According to the UN, early warning systems are a relatively low-cost investment that can have significant benefits. "The Global Commission on Adaptation estimated that a 24-hour notice of an impending disaster can reduce damage by 30 percent," it reports. "Investing $800 million in such systems in developing countries would prevent losses of $3 to $16 billion annually. With that in mind, the Early Warnings for All initiative advocates spending $3.1 billion from 2023 to 2027 to achieve universal coverage. That's equivalent to just 50 cents per person a year."[55] According to the UN, more than 75 percent of people now have cell phones, and even more can access the internet, making it even easier to reach a large number of people with an early warning system.

Take Action Now

> **"The earlier the adaptation measures are implemented, the more the world will benefit."[56]**
>
> —Intergovernmental Panel on Climate Change

It is widely agreed that there is a high degree of urgency when it comes to adaptation. The longer humanity waits, the more difficult and expensive adaptation is likely to be. Waiting is also likely to cause greater losses of life. The IPCC insists, "The earlier the adaptation measures are implemented, the more the world will benefit."[56] The UN stresses that although adaptation efforts are costly, the benefits of investing in adaptation will eventually be greater than the costs. It says, "Investing in adaptation makes a lot more sense than waiting and trying to catch up later. . . . Protecting people now saves more lives and reduces risks moving forward. It makes financial sense too because the longer we wait, the more the costs will escalate."[57] The UN says that waiting will not eliminate the need to adapt; instead, it will simply reduce potential benefits of being prepared.

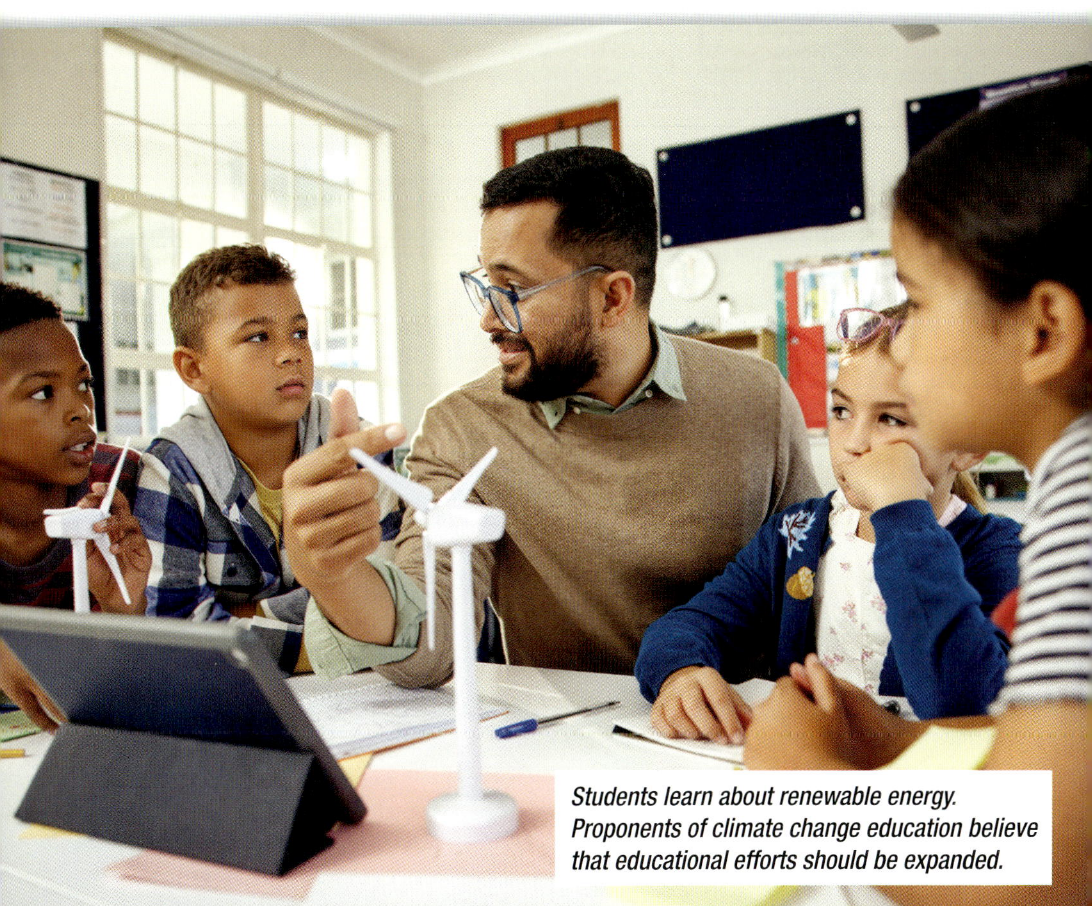

Students learn about renewable energy. Proponents of climate change education believe that educational efforts should be expanded.

As this list of needed actions shows, adapting to climate change will be a challenge for humanity, and most agree that meeting it will not be easy. However, evidence from around the world also reveals that there is hope. Joe Wegener of the Boston Consulting Group and Chitresh Saraswat of the World Economic Forum point out that human history is full of examples of successful adaptation in the face of overwhelming challenges. They state, "The story of human adaptation to the natural environment is as old as humans themselves."[58] Humanity has adapted many times before, and many are hopeful that it will be able to do so again.

SOURCE NOTES

Introduction: Adapting to Climate Change: A Critical Challenge

1. Quoted in Ronda Kaysen and Aatish Bhatia, "Nights in Las Vegas Are Becoming Dangerously Hot," *New York Times,* August 11, 2024. www.nytimes.com.
2. National Aeronautics and Space Administration, "Responding to Climate Change," June 2024. https://science.nasa.gov.
3. United Nations Framework Convention on Climate Change, Topics, introduction to "Adaptation and Resilience." https://unfccc.int.
4. National Aeronautics and Space Administration, "Responding to Climate Change."

Chapter One: Why Does Humanity Need to Adapt?

5. Quoted in Jon Hurdle, "As Climate Fears Mount, Some in U.S. Are Deciding to Relocate," *Yale Environment 360*, March 24, 2022. https://e360.yale.edu.
6. United Nations Development Programme, "What Is Climate Change Adaptation and Why Is It Crucial?," January 30, 2024. https://climatepromise.undp.org.
7. US Environmental Protection Agency, "Climate Change and Human Health," June 4, 2024. www.epa.gov.
8. Marina Romanello et al., "The 2023 Report of the *Lancet* Countdown on Health and Climate Change: The Imperative for a Health-Centred Response in a World Facing Irreversible Harms," *Lancet*, vol. 402, no. 10419, December 16, 2023. www.thelancet.com.
9. Intergovernmental Panel on Climate Change, "FAQ 4: How Are People Adapting to the Effects of Climate Change and What Are the Known Limits to Adaptation?," IPCC Sixth Assessment Report. www.ipcc.ch.
10. United Nations, "Climate Adaptation." www.un.org.
11. Aarti Lila Ram and Eric Shahzar, "Land, Loss and Liberation: Indigenous Struggles amid the Climate Crisis," World Economic Forum, February 9, 2024. www.weforum.org.

Chapter Two: What Actions Can Humanity Take to Adapt?

12. Quoted in Asian Environmental Youth Network, "Marinel Ubaldo: Rallying the People on the Frontlines of Climate Change," May 22, 2024. www.aeyn.org.

13. United Nations, "Water and Climate Change." www.unwater.org.
14. US Environmental Protection Agency, "Smart Growth and Climate Change," March 29, 2024. www.epa.gov.
15. US Environmental Protection Agency, "Heat Island Effect," August 2, 2024. www.epa.gov.
16. Quoted in World Meteorological Organization, *Early Warnings for All: The UN Global Early Warning Initiative for the Implementation of Climate Adaptation—Executive Action Plan, 2023–2027*. Geneva, Switzerland: World Meteorological Organization, 2022, p. 1. https://library.wmo.int/.
17. US Department of Agriculture, "Climate Change Adaptation." www.usda.gov.
18. Intergovernmental Panel on Climate Change, "FAQ 4."
19. World Wildlife Fund, "How WWF Is Preparing Mangroves for a New Climate Future," April 25, 2024. www.worldwildlife.org.

Chapter Three: Why Is Adaptation Challenging?

20. Calum Watson, "Glasgow: The Last Best Hope to Fight Climate Change," BBC News, October 29, 2021. https://www.bbc.co.uk.
21. National Aeronautics and Space Administration, "Responding to Climate Change."
22. United Nations Environment Programme, *Adaptation Gap Report 2023: Underfinanced. Underprepared. Inadequate Investment and Planning on Climate Adaptation Leaves World Exposed.* Nairobi: United Nations Environment Programme, 2023. www.unep.org.
23. Quoted in United Nations Environment Programme, *Adaptation Gap Report 2023*.
24. Quoted in Matthew Daly and Nuha Dolby, "Most in U.S. Want More Action on Climate Change, Says AP-NORC Poll," PBS News, October 26, 2022. www.pbs.org.
25. David G. Victor and Veerabhadran Ramanathan, "Opinion: Climate Change Isn't Just About Emissions. We're Ignoring a Huge Part of the Fight," *Los Angeles Times,* October 15, 2023. www.latimes.com.
26. Christiana Figueres, Yvo de Boer, and Michael Zammit Cutajar, "For 50 Years Governments Have Failed to Act on Climate Change. No More Excuses," *The Guardian*, June 2, 2022. www.theguardian.com.
27. Intergovernmental Panel on Climate Change, "FAQ 4."
28. Intergovernmental Panel on Climate Change, "FAQ 4."
29. Art Markman, "Why People Aren't Motivated to Address Climate Change," *Harvard Business Review,* October 11, 2018. https://hbr.org.

30. Quoted in Giancarlo Pasquini, Alison Spencer, Alec Tyson, and Cary Funk, "Why Some Americans Do Not See Urgency on Climate Change," Pew Research Center, August 9, 2023. www.pewresearch.org.
31. Quoted in Pasquini, Spencer, Tyson, and Funk, "Why Some Americans Do Not See Urgency on Climate Change."
32. Intergovernmental Panel on Climate Change, "FAQ 4."

Chapter Four: How Has Humanity Been Successful?

33. World Bank Group, "Key Highlights: Country Climate and Development Report for Bangladesh," October 31, 2022. www.worldbank.org.
34. Fatuma Hussein et al., "Understanding the Paris Agreement's 'Global Goal on Adaptation,'" World Resources Institute, February 1, 2024. www.wri.org.
35. Quoted in United Nations Environment Programme, "Drink Salty Water or Go Thirsty: Climate Change Hits Tanzanian School Children," February 14, 2019. www.unep.org.
36. Quoted in United Nations Environment Programme, "Drink Salty Water or Go Thirsty."
37. United Nations Environment Programme, "Darfur: Adapting to an Encroaching Desert," April 17, 2019. www.unep.org.
38. Quoted in Simone Stolzoff, "This Pacific Island Country Is Disappearing. What Happens Next?," *National Geographic,* July 8, 2024. www.nationalgeographic.com.
39. Loren Elliot and Kristy Needham, "Rising Sea Levels Are Forcing Fiji's Villagers to Relocate. They Want Polluters to Pay Instead," Reuters, August 1, 2022. www.reuters.com.
40. Quoted in Kate Lyons, "How to Move a Country: Fiji's Radical Plan to Escape Rising Sea Levels," *The Guardian,* November 8, 2022. www.theguardian.com.
41. UNDP Climate, "Colombia's Infinite Wetlands," June 25, 2021. https://undp-climate.exposure.co.
42. UNDP Climate, "Colombia's Infinite Wetlands."
43. Quoted in Joanna Adhem, "'Washed Away': Pakistan's Melting Glaciers Threaten Millions with Dangerous Flooding," Euro News, June 28, 2023. www.euronews.com.
44. UNDP Climate, "Melting Glaciers, Growing Lakes and the Threat of Outburst Floods," August 26. 2022. https://undp-climate.exposure.co.

Chapter Five:
What Actions Need to Be Taken in the Future?

45. European Environment Agency, "Europe Is Not Prepared for Rapidly Growing Climate Risks," March 10, 2024. www.eea.europa.eu.
46. Romanello, "The 2023 Report of the Lancet Countdown on Health and Climate Change."
47. Quoted in Madeline Ostrander, "Why We Can No Longer Afford to Ignore the Case for Climate Adaptation," *MIT Technology Review*, August 17, 2022. www.technologyreview.com.
48. World Health Organization, "Climate Change," October 12, 2023. www.who.int.
49. Mathilde Bouyé and David Waskow, "Climate Action Isn't Reaching the Most Vulnerable—but It Could," *Insights* (blog), World Resources Institute, November 11, 2021. www.wri.org.
50. United Nations Development Programme, "The Digital Age of Climate Change Adaptation," June 3, 2022. www.undp.org.
51. New Jersey Department of Environmental Protection, "Climate Change Education." https://dep.nj.gov.
52. Quoted in Hilary Howard, "Reading, Writing, Math . . . and Climate Change?" *New York Times*, January 22, 2024. www.nytimes.com.
53. U.S. Climate Resilience Toolkit, "Case Study: Luck Is Not a Policy We Can Count On: Boston Takes a Proactive Approach to Climate Adaptation," July 12, 2024. https://toolkit.climate.gov.
54. United Nations, "Finance & Justice." www.un.org.
55. United Nations, "Finance & Justice."
56. Intergovernmental Panel on Climate Change, "FAQ 4."
57. United Nations, "Climate Adaptation."
58. Joe Wegener and Chitresh Saraswat, "What History Can Teach Us About Climate Adaptation," World Economic Forum, September 19, 2023. www.weforum.org.

FOR FURTHER RESEARCH

Books

Editors of *Scientific American*, *Our Planet, Our Choice: The Science of Climate Change*. New York: Scientific American Educational, 2023.

Barry S. Levy and Jonathan A. Patz, eds., *Climate Change and the Public Health.* 2nd ed. New York: Oxford University Press, 2024.

Devi Lockwood, *1001 Voices on Climate Change: Everyday Stories of Flood, Fire, Drought, and Displacement from Around the World*. New York: Simon & Schuster Element, 2021.

Joseph J. Romm, *Climate Change: What Everyone Needs to Know.* New York: Oxford University Press, 2022.

Internet Sources

Global Center on Adaptation, "What Is Climate Adaptation?" https://gca.org.

Fatuma Hussein et al., "Understanding the Paris Agreement's 'Global Goal on Adaptation,'" *Insights* (blog) World Resources Institute, February 1, 2024. www.wri.org.

Marina Romanello et al., "The 2023 Report of the *Lancet* Countdown on Health and Climate Change: The Imperative for a Health-Centred Response in a World Facing Irreversible Harms," *Lancet*, vol. 402, no. 10419, December 16, 2023. www.thelancet.com.

United Nations Development Programme, "What Do People in Your Country Think?," Peoples' Climate Vote, 2024. https://peoplesclimate.vote/country-results.

World Health Organization, "Climate Change," October 12, 2023. www.who.int.

Raymond Zhong and Mira Rojanasakul, "How Close Are the Planet's Tipping Points?," *New York Times*, August 11, 2024. www.nytimes.com.

Organizations and Websites

Climate Change Adaptation Resource Center

www.epa.gov/arc-x

This website of the US Environmental Protection Agency provides information about climate change adaptation challenges and solutions in the United States. Users can search by issue and geographic area and will find articles about a wide variety of adaptation topics.

Global Center on Adaptation

https://gca.org

This international organization was founded in 2018 and is based in the Netherlands. It works to accelerate global adaptation to climate change. Its website contains reports and other information about climate change adaptation goals and progress around the world.

Intergovernmental Panel on Climate Change

www.ipcc.ch

This international organization was created in 1988 and publishes regular assessments on the effects of climate change. Its website provides these reports in addition to resources about adaptation options.

National Oceanic and Atmospheric Administration (NOAA)

www.noaa.gov

NOAA is a government agency that provides weather information, storm warnings, and climate monitoring. Its website has many articles about climate change and adaptation, including strategic plans for the future. It also has links to climate information from the National Weather Service.

UN Climate Change

https://unfccc.int

This United Nations website has a wide variety of information about climate change and adaptation, including news, case studies, and research papers. It also has information about international climate agreements.

INDEX

PICTURE CREDITS

Cover: Shutterstock

6: Associated Press
10: Ringo Chui/Shutterstock
13: Joerg Boethling/Alamy Stock Photo
16: paul kennedy/Alamy Stock Photo
19: Majority World CIC/Alamy Stock Photo
23: Chris Hellier/Alamy Stock Photo
26: Jake Lyell/Alamy Stock Photo
29: ungvar/Shutterstock
33: Kodo/Newscom
37: Shahidul Alam/Universal Images Group/Newscom
40: Wirestock, Inc./Alamy Stock Photo
43: Xinhua/Alamy Stock Photo
46: fokke baaressen/Shutterstock
50: Caroline Brehman/CQ Roll Call/Newscom
53: Rido/Shutterstock

ABOUT THE AUTHOR

Andrea C. Nakaya, a native of New Zealand, holds a bachelor's degree in English and a master's degree in communications from San Diego State University. She has written and edited numerous articles and more than fifty books on current issues. She currently lives in Eagle, Idaho.